Workbook for Becoming Unshakeable

By

Lysa S. Beltz

Copyright 2021 by Lysa Beltz and Women Empowered 4 Life, LLC.

All rights reserved. No part of this publication may be reproduced, distributed, or transmitted in any form or by any means, including photocopying, recording, or other electronic or mechanical methods, without the prior written permission of the publisher, except in the case of brief quotations embodied in critical reviews and certain other noncommercial uses permitted by copyright law. For permission requests, write to the publisher at the address below.

Unstoppable Publishing,
231 Public Square, Suite 300
Franklin, TN 37064

To protect the privacy of certain individuals, the names and identifying details have been changed.

Designations used by companies to distinguish their products are often claimed by trademarks. In all instances where the author or publisher is aware of a claim, the product names appear in Initial Capital letters. Readers, however, should contact the appropriate companies for more complete information regarding trademarks and registrations.

"Scripture quotations taken from the Amplified® Bible (AMP), Copyright © 2015 by The Lockman Foundation. Used by permission: www.Lockman.org

Unless otherwise indicated, all Scripture quotations are taken from THE MESSAGE, copyright © 1993, 2002, 2018 by Eugene H. Peterson. Used by permission of NavPress, Represented by Tyndale House Publishers. All rights reserved.

Scripture quotations marked TPT are from The Passion Translation®. Copyright © 2017, 2018 by Passion & Fire Ministries, Inc. Used by permission. All rights reserved. ThePassionTranslation.com.

Cover Design by Heather Hiatt
Editing by Laurel Lyford
Wheel of Life - Diagram - Coaching Tool in Black and White used with license from Shutterstock, created by Artellia, Royalty-free stock vector ID: 720019261

Unstoppable Publishing

ISBN: 978-1-7358589-8-2

Printed in the United States of America

Maybe the journey isn't so much about becoming anything. Maybe it's about un-becoming everything that isn't really you, so you can be who you were meant to be in the first place.

    -Unknown-

Table of Contents

BECOMING YOUR UNSHAKEABLE SELF 1

THE FOUNDATION 3

CHAPTER 1 - WHO AM I? 5
EXERCISE #1 PEACE THIEVES 5
EXERCISE #2 THE LIFE WHEEL 7
EXERCISE #3 CORE VALUES WORKSHEET 9
EXERCISE #4 FRUITS OF THE SPIRIT 11
EXERCISE #5 AFFIRMATIONS 12

CHAPTER 2 - WHO IS GOD, REALLY? 15
EXERCISE #6 WHAT DOES THE BIBLE SAY ABOUT GOD AS THE FATHER? 15
EXERCISE #7 WHO IS JESUS TO YOU? 19
EXERCISE #8 WHO IS THE HOLY SPIRIT TO YOU? 22

BECOMING MYSELF...23

CHAPTER 3 - THE DESTINATION 25
EXERCISE #9 DOES GOD HAVE A PLAN FOR ME? 25

CHAPTER 4 - DESTINY 27
EXERCISE #10 HERE ON PURPOSE FOR A PURPOSE 27

CHAPTER 5 - OBSTACLES 29
EXERCISE #11 THE OBSTACLE OF UNBELIEF 29
EXERCISE #12 THE OBSTACLE OF DOUBT 31
EXERCISE #13 THE OBSTACLE OF STRESS AND BUSYNESS 32

CHAPTER 6 - CHOICES AND DECISIONS 35
EXERCISE #14 WHAT DO YOU CHOOSE? 35

CHAPTER 7 - ANY AND EVERY ROAD 41
EXERCISE #15 WHAT DO YOU WANT? REALLY! 41

CHAPTER 8 - UNSHAKEABLE BEAUTY 43
EXERCISE #16 IT STARTS WITH A DECISION 43
EXERCISE #17 KINDNESS MATTERS 45

CHAPTER 9 - ABANDON THE UGLINESS 47
EXERCISE #18 FLYING BLIND 47

CHAPTER 10 - THE YOKE 49
EXERCISE #19 SO MANY ROCKS! 49

CHAPTER 11 - RESILIENCE 51
EXERCISE #20 LIFE IS FOR ME 51

CHAPTER 12 - PURITY OF HEART 53
EXERCISE #21 MOTIVATED 53

BECOMING UNSHAKEABLE **55**

CHAPTER 13 - IN STEP WITH THE HOLY SPIRIT **57**
EXERCISE #22 Why am I here? 57
EXERCISE #23 My Advocate 58
CHAPTER 14 - SUBMIT AND SURRENDER **59**
EXERCISE #24 What *do* I surrender? 59
CHAPTER 15 - WE ARE AN ENDANGERED SPECIES **61**
EXERCISE #25 The Power of Agreement 61
CHAPTER 16 BECOMING **63**
EXERCISE #26. God knows the how 63

BIBLIOGRAPHY **66**

INVITATION TO CONNECT **67**

ABOUT THE AUTHOR **68**

JOURNALING PAGES 69
.... 72

Becoming Your Unshakeable Self

Congratulations on ordering your workbook! This is an indicator that you are ready to work on Becoming your Unshakeable Self. The goal of the book and workbook is for you to realize how loved you are, that you are designed perfectly in the sight of God and that much of what holds you back is ready for you to let go of it.

This workbook is designed to work hand-in-hand with the book, *Becoming Unshakeable*. If you don't have a copy yet, I recommend you purchase the book before proceeding with the following exercises. There is detail in the book that will make the following chapters more meaningful for you.

We outgrow our mindsets, beliefs and self image as we mature and become who we are designed to be. It's important to do an occasional inventory and see where we are 'living in shoes two sizes too small'. When a sunflower seed is first planted, it can happily live in a small 2" terracotta pot with a little soil. As the plant buds and emerges and begins to grow taller, that tiny pot quickly becomes a restriction and will stunt the growth or kill the sunflower plant. To grow to 6 feet tall and support a large sunflower head, the plant needs deep roots, lots of soil and room to expand.

We are like that sunflower. When we are growing, if we try to remain in a small pot with too little soil, we will be inhibited to become who and what we are designed to be. Throughout the exercises in this book, I hope to challenge you to look at what you accept by default and eliminate the places that don't fit or support you any longer.

How to use this workbook successfully.

Do this work is for you alone. You are engaging in this work because you have value and you want to be and become exactly who you're meant to be so you can do all the things you are intended to do! You to have complete freedom to write the truth for you, as defined by you. Each exercise needs to be honest, truthful and real to be effective. If you feel like swearing, swear. If you need to cry, cry it out. If you are angry – be angry. Not to stay angry but to feel it, release it and grow from it. Writing superficial level work is not going to help you be unshakeable. Dig deep.

Most of my readers have found it effective to read through the entire *Becoming Unshakeable* book then come back and go through the workbook. That is only a suggestion however. You work the way and the pace that benefits you the most. Given that you don't have to read the book straight through, I recommend working on the chapters as you read them not necessarily in chronological order.

There is also room built into the workbook for recording your thoughts, ideas, breakthroughs, questions, etc. It's nice to have a place to jot things down when the inspiration strikes.

Knowing how life can impact our ability to complete things, be sure to write yourself a note where you left off and what your current a-ha! was, so you can more easily resume where you left off. It's OK if completing the workbook takes days, weeks, months or even years. Give yourself permission and grace to keep at it. You will be drawn to the right chapter and exercise at exactly the right time. Trust the process!

I would love to hear about your experience with the workbook – what touched you the most, brought the greatest breakthrough and made you dig the deepest. Send me an email at CoachLysa@lysabeltz.com. I can't wait to hear from you!

Part 1

THE FOUNDATION

Chapter 1 - WHO AM I?

Exercise #1 Peace Thieves

Life can be chaotic and unpredictable. There are many issues that can steal our peace and keep us from being unshakeable if we allow them to. Take the next 5 minutes and do a brain dump - a listing of all the things in your life that create worry, concern, fear or anxiety. Just write until you exhaust the list. Keep in mind, we get more of what we focus on, so we are not going to remain focused on these, but we need to acknowledge they exist.

Unshakeable Thought: If you have no control over an issue and you cannot influence the outcome, it is wasted energy to worry about it and allow it to become bigger than it should. For example, I cannot control or influence the possibility of an asteroid hitting the earth. I can control what food I put into my mouth.

Look at the list you generated. Circle the items you CAN control or at a minimum influence the outcome. Draw a line through all the items that are outside your control. What is the % of issues you circled? These are the items that MAY deserve your attention. The others are candidates to be cut loose and let go of.

Of the circled items listed above, what are the top 3 issues that you genuinely have control over? I recommend you select the 3 that are robbing your peace on a frequent basis. We will continue to refer to and address these issues throughout the workbook.

1.

2.

3.

Exercise #2 The Life Wheel

When I think about myself, I see a network of relationships, thoughts, activities, desires, fears, hurts, mountains, and valleys, and it gets overwhelming. We are complex creatures as human beings. I am a daughter, a friend, a wife, a mother, an employee, a project manager, a writer, etc. and I am just me. Our lives are so demanding that it is very easy to feel like all I do is spin plates and scramble to keep any of the important ones from crashing and shattering.

I want to introduce a tool called the Life Balance Wheel or Life Wheel. This helps you evaluate the different areas and aspects of your life to see where you are balanced or out of balance. It can also show you where you are satisfied or unsatisfied in your life so you can determine where to take steps to change.

Steps to complete the Life Wheel:
1. Look at the categories or headings on the chart. Are there areas of your life that are not represented? Exchange your idea for one of the existing headings.
2. For each category, evaluate on a scale of 1 – 10 (1 = highly dissatisfied and 10 = highly satisfied) where you currently rate your life.
3. Complete each section thoughtfully and be sure to respond to how life is, not what you want it to be.

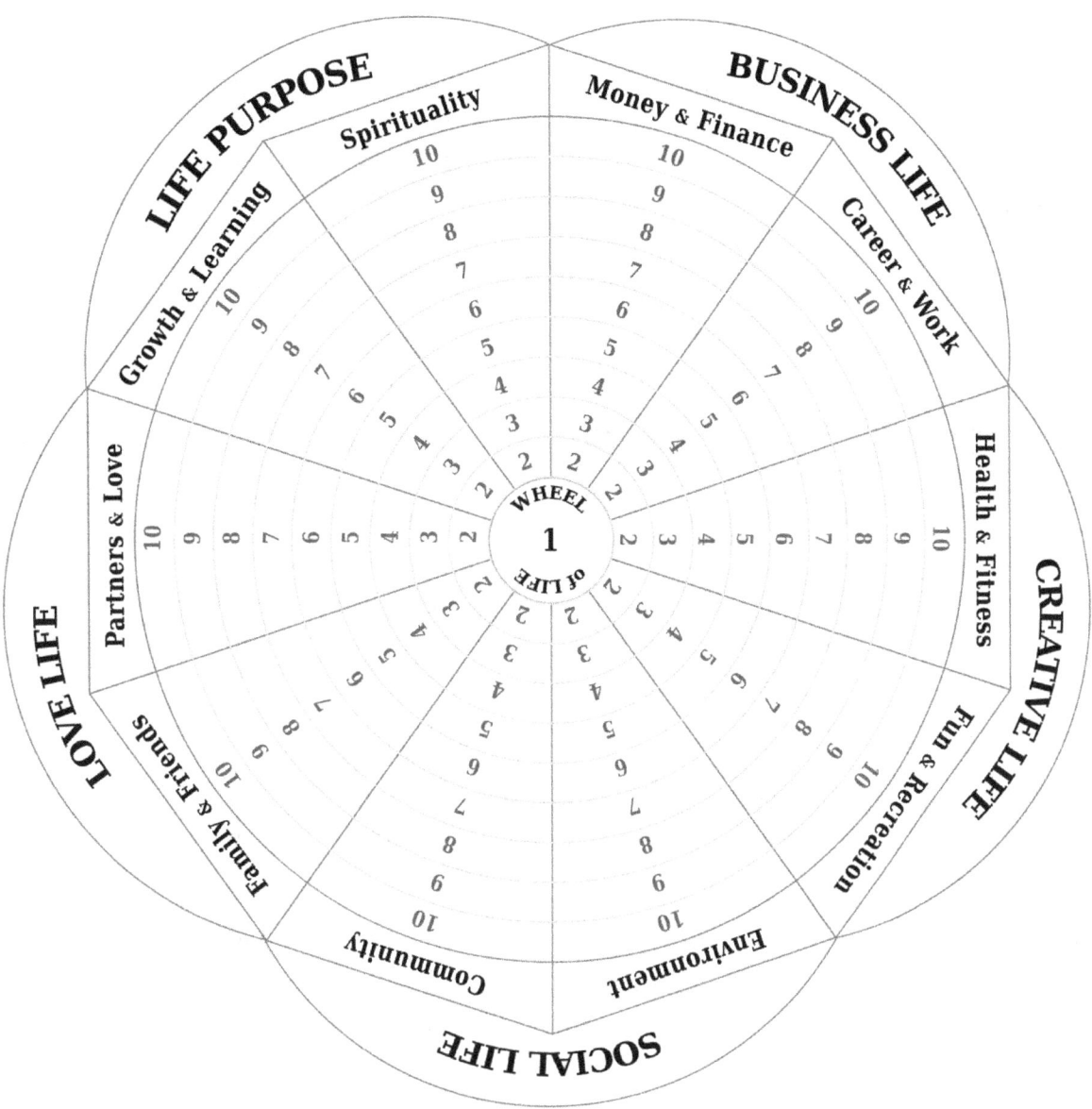

The power of the Life Wheel is a visible representation of your reality. Knowing we cannot effectively work on all areas at the same time, this gives you an approach to pick a category that is out-of-balance and begin to work on it.

If you are more visual, use different colored pens to fill in the categories by coloring them from the middle out. You can also circle the numbers or just draw a line to show where you're at. Since you have the .pdf of this document, you can also revisit this exercise in 3 or 6 months to see what has changed and make a new valuation of where to invest your focus.

Exercise #3 Core Values Worksheet

Each of us is designed and created by God with intrinsic core values. These are our internal bottom lines of what has and brings value to our life. The quote, "Give me liberty or give me death" is an example of Patrick Henry's impassioned cry just prior to the Revolutionary War. Freedom, or liberty, was a core value that he was willing to fight for and to die for. You are *"Fearfully and wonderfully made "*, according to Psalm 139 and that includes your personal core values.

The following exercise has no right or wrong answers. This is 100% about what is important to you. The list of words is also a starting place – it is not all inclusive. If you have values that are important to you, add them to the list in the blank spaces.

Values Worksheet

Start by selecting 15 values, and then narrow your selection down to five values.

Achieving	Enthusiastic	Imagination	Performance
Action-oriented	Equality	Influential	Perseverance
Appreciation	Ethical	Informative	Personable
Authenticity	Excellence	Innovation	Power
Beauty	Expertise	Integrity	Professionalism
Benevolent	Faith	Joyful	Quality
Biblical Values	Faithful	Justice	Recognition
Camaraderie	Family	Kindness	Relationships
Careful	Fearless	Knowledge	Resourceful
Caring	Forgiveness	Learning	Respect
Community	Fun	Legacy	Results-Oriented
Compassion	Generous	Love	Safety
Competence	Gentleness	Loyalty	Security
Continuous Learning	Genuine	Mastery	Spiritual
Courage	Gratitude	Meaningful	Stability
Creativity	Happy	Merciful	Strength
Creditable	Hard Work	Nurturing	Teamwork
Dedicated	Health	Obedience	Trust
Dependable	Helpful	Optimistic	Truth
Determined	Honesty	Orderly	Unity
Efficiency	Honorable	Organization	Virtuous
Encouragement	Hope	Peace	Wisdom
Energetic	Humility	Perfection	Youthful

Select 10 Values	Select 5 Values
1.	1.
2.	2.
3.	3
4.	4.
5.	5
6.	Hint: What is unmovable for you? Where do you draw a line and will not cross it?
7.	
8.	
9.	
10.	
Hint: where do your peace and your passion lie?	

Your 5 core values typically do not change throughout your life. They partially define who you are and what makes you tick (and get ticked off!). It is very telling to have your significant other, friends and children do this same exercise. It often highlights why you and they see and feel differently about things.

When you look back at the Life Wheel exercise, you may see a correlation between areas that are not satisfactory and your core values. When we are in circumstances, jobs or relationships that violate or go against our core values, it creates discomfort. You have to prayerfully evaluate what God would have you do to adjust, change or fix the situation. Sometimes He gives us grace to walk through that situation and teaches us to rely on Him. Other times He will show you a better direction to go.

Exercise #4 Fruits of the Spirit

Just as each of us is designed with core values, we also have spiritual gifts placed within us. Scripturally we are told that everyone of us is born with spiritual gifts. If you don't know what yours are, you still have them. Below is a list of the gifts as most people define them:

List of 23 spiritual gifts:
1. Administration and Ruling
2. Apostleship / Pioneering
3. Craftsmanship
4. Creative Communication
5. Discernment
6. Encouraging /Exhorting
7. Evangelism
8. Faith
9. Giving
10. Healing
11. Hospitality
12. Intercession (prayer)
13. Interpretation
14. Knowledge
15. Leadership
16. Mercy
17. Miracles
18. Prophecy / Perceiving
19. Pastor / Shepherding
20. Serving/Ministry
21. Tongues
22. Teaching
23. Wisdom

The basis for the list comes from 4 different sections of the bible:
Romans 12:6-8
1 Corinthians 12:8-10
1 Corinthians 12:28-30
Ephesians 4:11

If you go to Google or any of the search engines and enter 'Free Spiritual Gifts Test' you will find a few different tests. I recommend doing a couple of them to get different perspectives. If you don't like any of those, I have one I use and I can send you a link to it for a fee. ($15-$25 depending on which test you choose.) Contact me via email at CoachLysa@LysaBeltz.com and use the Subject Line "Spiritual Gifts Test".

Exercise #5 Affirmations

An affirmation is a statement about you, your life, or your circumstances. You say and think affirmations every day. Studies have shown that we think up to approximately 60,000 thoughts a day and about 80% of those are negative. When we intentionally write and speak *positive* affirmations, we begin to shift the belief system in our heads. Over time, we can retrain our brains – we, literally, rewire how our brains think and process information. When we use God's Word as the basis for our affirmations, it begins to get powerful. I have found for myself that I must speak them out loud to get the most effect from affirmations. There is something that happens when you hear your own voice affirming yourself. It is also great to post a couple on your bathroom mirror, so you see them in the morning. It's really helpful to repeat them out loud multiple times a day, especially when you are first getting started and working on creating the mental shift. It may feel funny at first to say things out loud, but I promise you, it works!

Here are details and examples on how to write powerful affirmations – format, intent, what not to write, etc.

Examples of good affirmations:

- Self-Image:
    - I matter.
    - I am enough.
    - I claim and own my power to do good in the world.
    - I move in excellence not perfection.

- Finances:
    - My God supplies my need.
    - I am financially sound and able to give generously.
    - I am wise with money.

- Mental Health:
    - I give grace to myself.
    - I am clear-minded and focused.
    - I am loved and accepted.
    - I have all the will power and determination I need to accomplish my goals.
    - I have pure and genuine intentions.

- Health:
    - I am well able to do all that God has called me to do.
    - My health improves daily, and I have all the energy and wellbeing I need to live an abundant life.
    - I am healthy and at my perfect weight and size to accomplish all I am designed to do.

- Time Management:
    - I use my time wisely and effectively.
    - I have all the time I need to successfully complete my priorities each and every day.

- Abundance:
    - I am an overcomer.
    - I open my mind, heart, and spirit to receive abundance.
    - Miracles come to me freely and easily from sources known and unknown, expected and unexpected.
    - I expand in abundance, success and love everyday as I inspire those around me to do the same.
    - I am a magnet to abundant and blissful miracles daily.

- Business:
    - I am blessed and favored in business.
    - Everything I set my hand to produces fruit and reaps a great harvest.
    - The Lord is on my side and is for me and is opening doors for me every day.

A good affirmation is a strong statement that begins with "I" or "I am". It is always present tense, positive, specific, actionable and inspiring. It states how you want life to be, never what you don't want. It is in line with what you really want in life – your top priorities. We get more of what we focus on so always affirm the positive.

Examples of poor affirmations.
1. I don't eat emotionally.
    a. Instead say, "I am healthy and energetic. I only eat clean and nutritious foods to fuel my energy and my joy".
2. I make mistakes all the time!
    a. Instead say, "I am fully capable and competent at my job".
3. I want to pay off all my debt.
    a. Instead say, "I am making positive steps every day towards financial freedom.

The real power with an affirmation is how it makes you feel - - that is more important than the words themselves. You may need to try a few different statements to find *the* ones(s) that really resonate with you. It needs to make you feel empowered, overcoming and fully capable as you repeat the statement.

Referring back to Exercise #1, pick your top 3 Peace Thieves and let's re-write those with Positive affirmations.

1.

2.

3.

Finally, make a commitment to repeat the affirmations out loud at least twice a day for 14 days. Post them on your mirror, computer or wherever they will uplift and encourage you. The important thing is to keep them visible.

Chapter 2 - WHO IS GOD, REALLY?

Exercise #6 What does the Bible say about God as the Father?

As mentioned in the text of the book, regardless of how good or bad your relationship with your earthly father or dad was, God is a good Father and is in fact the standard for what a father is supposed to be. The following scriptures will help you dig deeper into what the bible says about Him as Father.

> (Psalm 68:5-6) (TPT)
> *To the fatherless he is a father.*
> *To the widow he is a champion friend.*
> *The lonely he makes part of a family.*
> *The prisoners he leads into prosperity until they sing for joy.*
> *This is our Holy God in his Holy Place!*

Which of these phrases do you relate to? Spend time thinking about how you would like to relate to the Father.

Matthew 6:25-26 (TPT)

> ²⁵ *"This is why I tell you to never be worried about your life, for all that you need will be provided, such as food, water, clothing—everything your body needs. Isn't there more to your life than a meal? Isn't your body more than clothing?*
>
> ²⁶ *"Consider the birds—do you think they worry about their existence? They don't plant or reap or store up food, yet your heavenly Father provides them each with food. Aren't you much more valuable to your Father than they?* ²⁷ *So, which one of you by worrying could add anything to your life?*

What are you worried about in your life that God has already said He will provide? Identify at least one thing you will quit worrying about and give to Him in faith.

Matthew 7:11 (TPT)

> ¹¹ *If you, imperfect as you are, know how to lovingly take care of your children and give them what's best, how much more ready is your heavenly Father to give wonderful gifts to those who ask him?"*

Pick one of the following questions to answer:
1. What is your favorite memory of something your father or a father figure gave to you?
2. What is your favorite memory of something you gave to your child/children?
3. What is one key thing you wish you had received as a gift. Write out a description of Father God giving that to you.

There is a story in the book of Luke about the 'Prodigal Son'. The younger son of a rich man asked for his inheritance and ran off to seek the world. After time had passed, he squandered all the money and was living in a pig sty, starving. He decided to return home and ask to be a servant where he knew he would at least get fed. Here is the description of the son coming home and the father's reaction. This is the same way God feels about each of us when we come back into relationship with Him.

> *Luke 15:20.* [20] *"So the young son set off for home. From a long distance away, his father saw him coming, dressed as a beggar, and great compassion swelled up in his heart for his son who was returning home. The father raced out to meet him, swept him up in his arms, hugged him dearly, and kissed him over and over with tender love.*

If there has been a distance between you and the Father, now is a perfect time to mend that. Even if you are open to and close to the Father, how can you deepen your relationship with Him? Write out your thoughts, desires and ideas for your relationship with the Father.

Here are several additional scriptures for you to read through.

Rom 8:15

15 And you did not receive the "spirit of religious duty," leading you back into the fear of never being good enough. But you have received the "Spirit of full acceptance," enfolding you into the family of God. And you will never feel orphaned, for as he rises up within us, our spirits join him in saying the words of tender affection, "Beloved Father!"

2 Cor 6:18

*I will be a true Father to you,
and you will be my beloved sons and daughters,"
says the Lord Yahweh Almighty.*

Eph 1:3-6

3 Every spiritual blessing in the heavenly realm has already been lavished upon us as a love gift from our wonderful heavenly Father, the Father of our Lord Jesus—all because he sees us wrapped into Christ. This is why we celebrate him with all our hearts!

4 And in love he chose us before he laid the foundation of the universe! Because of his great love, he ordained us, so that we would be seen as holy in his eyes with an unstained innocence.

5–6 For it was always in his perfect plan to adopt us as his delightful children, through our union with Jesus, the Anointed One, so that his tremendous love that cascades over us would glorify his grace—for the same love he has for the Beloved, Jesus, he has for us. And this unfolding plan brings him great pleasure!

Jesus

We have so much history to look back on and to see how Jesus has been portrayed, understood and misunderstood for two centuries. Is He still relevant in the 21st century? What role does He want to play in my life and what role do I want Him to play? Can I trust Him with my deepest secret longings, with my doubts and fears and of course, can He overlook all the mistakes I've made?

Exercise #7 Who is Jesus to you?

There are as many experiences with God as there are people reading this book. Each of us have a different personal awareness and experience with Jesus. What I perceive and experience does not necessarily equal what's real. When you wanted a dog or cat as a child and your parents said No, it wasn't because they didn't love you. There were other circumstances that you couldn't see or understand because of where you were in life. Jesus is the same. When our prayers are not answered at all or answered in a very different way than we expected, we can become resentful or angry or even just walk away. There is a need to trust that He has our best interests at heart. When that trust is present, we are far more open to believing that He will bring us good things.

Jesus will never be offended by truthful, honest questions. What DO you think about Jesus today? Does He have a place in your life? Do you want Him to have a place in your life? I assume yes since you are reading this workbook. Regardless of anything you've done in your past, called Jesus in the past, used His name as a swear word, etc., NONE of that has to affect your relationship with Jesus from this time forward. If you're not sure He's really real, ask Him to show you something irrefutable that will convince you He's there and He cares for you. (Remember, what you ask has to be in alignment with His love and character).

Take a few minutes and get deeply honest about your perception of Jesus. First, look in the rear-view mirror and see what it looks like there. Did you cry out to Him at one time and never got an answer? Did you pray earnestly for something and it didn't come about, and you blame Him? Did He seem to answer prayers when you were little but then it stopped? Or did you have a good relationship with Him, but life drifted you away?

What experiences, good and bad have shaped your beliefs about Jesus?
What do you want your relationship with Him to be like going forward?

Who is Jesus to you?

The Holy Spirit

The Holy Spirit is the third person of the Godly Trinity and in our lives as believers, the Holy Spirit brings the completion of God in our lives. All three persons of the Godhead have always existed so it's not like the Holy Spirit was an afterthought or came late to the party. The Holy Spirit is our teacher, guide, inner small voice, cheerleader, coach, corrections officer, and, most importantly, our best friend. The Holy Spirit is constantly drawing us upwards, toward the Father, towards our higher purpose. What He sees is the person God always intended you to be – how He perfectly designed you in His image with gifts, talents, and abilities that were always intended for good. THIS is the real you. When you peel back all the layers of gunk that have accumulated on you over time, the person you ARE is still there. God has never lost sight of YOU even when you have.

Sidetrack: I am a bit of a geek (ok, a lot) and I love numbers. God speaks to me in numbers frequently. Let's do a little bible number trivia about the number 3. In Pastor Troy Brewer's book, *Numbers that Preach*, he tells us that the number three represents "Perfect Completion".

Here are examples of the number 3 in the bible from that same book:

1. On the third day of creation, God created land. (Gen 1:9)
2. God told Moses to have the people of Israel be ready for His visitation on the third day. (Exodus 19:11)
3. There were 3 crosses on the hill when Jesus was crucified, it was at the 3rd hour, and there were three hours of darkness when he died.
4. Peter denied Jesus' three times.
5. Jesus rose on the third day.
6. Peter proclaimed his love for Jesus three times after the resurrection.

We can read about many more examples of the number three and a lot of other numbers that have been researched for centuries. God is a master mathematician and it literally does all add up!

Exercise #8 Who is the Holy Spirit to you?

John 16:7 (TPT) *But here's the truth: It's to your advantage that I (Jesus) go away, for if I don't go away the Divine Encourage will not be released to you. But after I depart, I will send him to you.*

When Jesus was preparing to return to Heaven, his friends, the disciples, were very sad to know he was really leaving them. They had lost Him once and were heartbroken to lose Him a second time. Jesus explained to them how necessary it was for him to go so that the Holy Spirit could come and be with all of them, all the time, simultaneously.

The same is true for us today. When we invite Jesus into our lives, we also immediately get the companionship of the Holy Spirit. We are told that our bodies are where the Holy Spirit dwells on earth. He is within each of us, all the time, every day. He doesn't take weekends off. ☺

Here are more scriptures that describe who the Holy Spirit is and how He operates in our lives. I encourage you to read them over a couple of times and then write below what your thoughts are about Him, how you will interact with Him and any questions you have. He will show you the answers when you are ready for them. It's fine to do an online search if that's easier for you.

John 14:26, Romans 8:14, Romans 8:26, Ephesians 4:30, 1 Corinthians 2:10-14, 1 Corinthians 3:16 Ephesians 2:22, Matthew 28:19, 20

Other names of the Holy Spirit: Holy Ghost, Comforter, symbol of the dove, breath of God, from the beginning, breathed life into Adam, let him breathe new life into you. Advocate, Intercessor--Counselor, Strengthener.

Part 2

BECOMING MYSELF

Chapter 3 - THE DESTINATION

A man makes his plans, but the Lord God establishes them" (Prov 16:9).

Exercise #9 Does God have a plan for me?

Refer back to the story of Joseph in Genesis 39. What would have appeared to be a significant detour in his journey to becoming was a training and proving ground for the profound plan that God had in place all the while.

What bothers you the most about *your* journey? Is it the hardships, the seeming insignificance of where you are and what you're doing, the mistakes you've made, the attacks others have made on you or your dreams? Each of us will have our experiences and circumstances in life. We can either choose to trust that we are right on track or we can allow negativity to rob us of important lessons that contribute to the total picture of who we are becoming in Jesus.

God DOES have a plan for your life. Jeremiah 29:11 says it this way:

"For I know the plans I have for you, plans to give you a hope and a future."

The antidote to unbelief is gratitude and praise for God. When my eyes are on His glory and I stop and recount all the marvelous things God has done for me, it will hush the critic that wants to complain so loudly. Your eyes can only look in one place at a time; choose wisely where you have your focus.

1. What are your natural <u>skills and abilities</u> that you know are God-designed in you? Everyone has them – do not let yourself off the hook on this question. You DO have natural talents that God will use. I encourage you to write down at least three.

2. Write down what you want the future to look like as far as your <u>attitude and approach</u> to using your natural talents to create a better future.

Chapter 4 - DESTINY

Exercise #10 Here on purpose for a purpose

The purpose of this exercise is to look at your destiny as being just as significant in our day as Joseph's was in his. If you are following the journey that God has offered to you, you're in an important place. It sounds trite to say that you are the only you, but it is so true! No one else has the life experience that you've had to put you right in the place where you are, with the knowledge you have, or to speak to the exact people that you come in contact with.

1. You are here on purpose and for a purpose. Write down what you know of that purpose including any new impressions you have while reading this book. Include questions that come to mind that you need to think about or journal about.

2. Part of stepping into an Unshakeable Life is being brutally honest with yourself about what you're *good* at and what you know deep inside you are made to do. Digging deep, what does your spirit, the Holy Spirit, and your intuition – that inner knowing – tell you about your purpose? Write down exactly what comes to you – don't edit it in your head. Just let it flow.

Chapter 5 - OBSTACLES

Exercise #11 The Obstacle of Unbelief

Unbelief is a hindrance to seeing our prayers answered. God understands when we have doubt and hesitation, but unbelief is unacceptable to Him. Jesus left the splendor of the heavenly realm and the continual presence of the Father to humble himself and come to earth as a human man, knowing that He would be the ultimate sacrificial Lamb. When I live or move in unbelief, it makes the sacrifice mean nothing. God forgives us because every one of us has done this at some point in time in our lives. The word repent means to 'think again' or 'think differently'.

Spend 15 – 20 minutes or longer and really dig into your unbelief. Look for emotions tied or related to the unbelief. Is there grief, anger, remorse, regret, fear, or anything else? Are there certain memories or events that surface when you think about why you can't or don't believe something about God? Often our events and reactions from earlier in our lives, even childhood or adolescence can become a buried emotion which grows into a belief system even when we don't know why.

When I was around age five, I had a piggy bank that was a pig in a sailor suit and hat. I remember really loving that bank. It fell on the ground and broke. I remember asking my mom, "Why did God let that happen?". I was broken-hearted. As an adult, I found the emotion of distrust was buried deep in my memory bank and it was hard for me to trust God with certain aspects of my finances.

Trust that whatever thoughts, emotions or memories come to mind are popping up for a reason. Ask the Holy Spirit to show you and then write down whatever comes to mind – don't overthink it and don't reject any emotions that surface.

The Obstacle of Unbelief

Exercise #12 The Obstacle of Doubt

What is the difference between doubt and unbelief? The dictionary defines doubt as:

"A feeling of uncertainty or lack of conviction."

To move from doubt to belief, we have to learn to think differently. We have to choose to learn to think about things the way God does. We learn to do this by reading His word and asking the Holy Spirit to open our understanding of how to apply His Word in our everyday lives. We talk about 'coming into alignment' with God's Word. It is learning to value what God values and look at ourselves the way He does – with grace and love.

The serpent asked a 'simple' question – "Has God truly said…?" Satan planted the first seed of doubt and when that seed germinated, all the other negative emotions blossomed along with it: fear, disbelief, depression, loneliness, separateness, pain – physical and emotional, etc. What seeds of doubt have been planted in the garden of your mind? What lingering questions keep you from fully engaging with God in your life? Can you identify negative emotions and questions that make you just not feel good or right about yourself or your relationship with God?

The Obstacle of Doubt

Exercise #13 The Obstacle of Stress and Busyness

Our 'normal' life contains far more stress that is imposed on us or we impose on ourselves than I believe God ever intended us to have. So many of us, me included, add artificial and unnecessary stress on top of that. It's the stress from credit card debt. The stress of having 3 kids in 3 different sports at 3 different fields across town at the same time (not knocking sports here!). The stress of not getting enough sleep because you're hooked on that Netflix series and stayed up to 1 a.m. watching it. The stress of overcommitting to good things – church activities, volunteer opportunities, being on the Homeowners Association board, and the list can go on and on and on.

Identify areas of your life where you have voluntarily opened the door to added stress. The goal here is to recognize it and identify it so you can make decisions around what you want going forward. You are in control of your life – you are not a passenger. You get to CHOOSE what you do and do not let yourself off the hook with excuses. Important Note: Not all added stress is bad or unnecessary. You may have chosen something because you love it or it's the right thing to do.

For each stressor in your life, complete the following:
1. What is the stress situation?
2. Did you intentionally choose it to start with?
    a. If yes, why? What core value does it satisfy and how does it impact your life wheel?
    b. If no, what core value did you violate by not saying no and what is the impact on your life wheel?
3. What is your action plan going forward?
    a. Ideas here are things like:
        i. Keep this commitment for the value it brings to my life.
        ii. Complete the term of the commitment for now but do not re-up next time. (Make a firm plan ahead of time for saying no. You can do an affirmation around it.)
        iii. Decide you really do not have time/energy/finances for the situation and generate your exit strategy.
            1. Be clear with yourself that you are making this change to increase and improve your quality of life, your mental health and sanity or even your physical health.
            2. Others may be disappointed with your decision, but they are not living your life.

List as many stressors as you identify and answer the questions for each one.

The obstacle of stress and busyness

Chapter 6 - CHOICES AND DECISIONS

Exercise #14 What do you choose?

Choices face us every day and it's in the moment-by-moment, split-second decisions that our life's journey is played out. When Jesus needed to make important decisions, He got alone with the Father and poured his heart out to the One who loved him most. Jesus's heart was to accomplish the perfect will of the Father. Only through ongoing, personal conversation – talking and listening, could Jesus correctly discern the perfect will of the Father. God wants us to know His will for our lives. He does not keep it hidden nor does He want you to have to strive and search and search and search to find it. He will sometimes only reveal a portion of our future but that is done out of love to not overwhelm us.

When we can't find what is 'right', it can be because we are not openly listening, or we go into asking with an agenda and an outcome we already believe is what we should do. Or, as so many of us do, we make a decision without asking and then ask Him to bless it or ask what happened when it goes sideways.

He has walked me through more minefields of my own making than I care to recount. Every single time the outcome of asking for His help has provided a way through that was far better than what I ever thought I could ask for. Our God does not do things half-way. You are redeemed fully, not partially. You are saved fully, you are loved fully – flaws, faults, imperfections, skinned knees, and all.

This brings us back to the topic of God's perfect will/plan, His permissive will/plan, or being *out* of His will/plan. Let's start with looking at where you might be out of His Plan.

When we intentionally or accidentally go where we are not supposed to be, there are always warning signs – usually several of them. A deep, inner knowing or suspicion that something isn't right. I have several girlfriends who knew before and the day of their weddings that this was not the right guy. To save embarrassment or thinking it was just them second-guessing, they continued into the marriage only to have it fall apart in a few years or less. Other signs we may encounter include getting chills or repeating thoughts, or you have a lack of peace about something.

We can intentionally make choices and decisions that we know from the start will not end well. You might call this rebellion or self-sabotage. **It is where you knowingly do what you consider to be wrong.** As teenagers, we rebel in order to find our own boundaries and to pull away and become independent. As adults, the behaviors can look the same yet the heart motivation behind the actions and choices can be far more impacting. Rebellion can run up thousands of dollars on a credit card in short order. It can also open the door to substance abuse. (Note: This is different than self-expression or embracing the fact that you think differently than others.) Self-sabotage is often rooted in feeling you don't deserve something. We make bad choices in the subconscious hope that we will not exceed what we think we deserve.

Think and journal about when you have operated from a wrong motivation and it still bugs you. This means there is unresolved emotion there that you need to take a look at. Once you've written about it, ask God what to do to resolve it. Some possibilities might be to ask Him to forgive you, seek forgiveness from the other person, forgive yourself, call up that other person and check in on them and work to mend the relationship. The important thing is to release and resolve what still bothers you or hurts your heart.

Being in the permissive plan of God means I'm generally headed in the right direction for the right reasons. I then take a few detours along the way and detours become my way of doing life. It can be the three-steps-forward-and-two-steps-back or it can look like the map here or any combination of ups and downs, forwards and backwards or just being stuck and not moving at all.

There tends to be repeating patterns where we do good and great for a period time, then things slip a bit, we spin around like a red Datsun pickup on solid ice and go off the road backwards. (Literally me, twice!) We struggle for some period of time and slowly get back on track and go after life again. Sound familiar?

Look for your patterns and what triggers you to get off track. Is it a person, a season of the year, the anniversary of someone's death, holidays, boredom, overwhelm, self-judgment or self-hatred, criticism from someone? Knowledge is power. Identifying your triggers and your repeating patterns is the first step towards taking control of that part of your life. You can lessen or eliminate the déjà vu when you have a plan before it happens again.

Write or draw what you know or can identify of your pattern(s). How often do they repeat? Are there warning signs that you can use as cues to take the offensive and head them off? Can you ask someone to be an accountability partner ahead of time? Be creative and be your own best friend. This is intended to set you free, not put more guilt or heaviness in place.

When we are following Gods BEST plan, we are 'In the Flow'. Life is happening for us not to us.

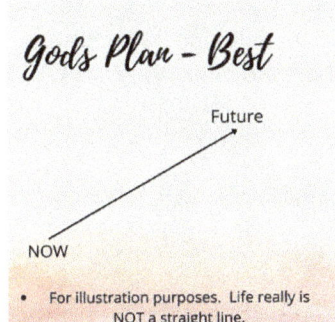

There is a rhyme and a rhythm to life. It just feels different. You have goals and are working towards them consistently. When the bad things happen, you are able to deal with them head-on and pivot as needed. You remain optimistic even though circumstances are less than fabulous. You are in touch and in tune with the Divine daily and your prayers are effective, and you are seeing answers to them regularly. Life is good. You still have slips and dips – we are perfectly imperfect after all, but they don't throw you into a tailspin (like my red Datsun pickup).

Is it possible to stay in this mode always? Yes, and no. The Holy Spirit is always with us. We are where He lives. He is unchanging and never leaves us. He is our teacher, counselor, guide, cheerleader and also disciples us and brings correction as needed. We can have a lifestyle that is 100% sold out for God. We talk about being "All In!". This is the best way to be in my experience.

The no part is, we are human, and we can get hit with life or challenges or illness that impacts us in major ways. I do not want you to set an expectation for yourself that is impossible to live up to. We are still learning, growing, evolving, discovering and becoming. God will ask us to learn something new or come up to a new level and it's HARD. I think of life as a marathon not a sprint. To go for the longer distances, it takes a lot of practice and training and perhaps some pain and a twisted ankle or two. We keep moving forward at our own perfect pace, keeping an eye on the prize to fulfilling our life purpose.

We can be in-the-flow in parts of our lives and not others. I may have my finances on track, but my health management is off. I can do great on eating clean, but my sleep schedule is messed up. My heart motivation can be on track, but my mind is struggling with inadequacy. Then there are times when all cylinders are tuned to perfection and we feel Unshakeable at every level. This is when life is just FUN.

Use this time and space to refer back to your Life Balance Wheel and the different categories you used. For each one, identify what it felt like when you were 'in the flow' and all was good. What was happening around you, for you, what did you feel, what were you doing in that period of time? If we can identify what was working so right, it helps us be able to intentionally recreate that and also increase the frequency of life being that way.

Chapter 7 - ANY AND EVERY ROAD

Exercise #15 What do you want? Really!

One of the quotes I use is from the Cheshire Cat in Alice in Wonderland, "When you don't know where you are going, any road will get you there."

When God asked me what *I* wanted; I didn't have an answer. I'm not used to being asked that question. I had to work through it for a while to really decide what I did want. Part of the puzzle is also knowing what you don't want. Some things I identified that are not what I want more of came from mistakes I made. However, God does not waste our experiences but redeems them all for His glory. "I never lose. I either win or I learn". (Nelson Mandela)

God's ways are simple; Be who He made you. Like what you like, love what you love, do what you're good at – and do it in relationship with Him. When we have hearts that love God and we want to be in a good relationship with Him, life gets way easier.

So far in your life, have you defaulted to taking any old road that came along? Or do you pick your road with intention? I lived so much of my life feeling like I accepted whatever road came along. I was not in the driver's seat of my life. Now, I am alive with intention and choosing wisely which road I take and ensuring that God agrees with my plans and that He and I are co-creating together. It is far more fun and rewarding this way.

To begin to live with intention, start by thinking about what you want out of life. For this exercise, think about what you want to have accomplished one year from today? If you have a calendar on your phone, put in a reminder in 3, 6, 9 months and a year from now so you will be prompted to think and live with intention along the way.   Ask God to give you an idea of what is really possible for you. Again, write down the first things that come to mind no matter how far-fetched they may seem. Trust that what is coming to you is God-inspired. (Because it is!)

Think big, dream big and plan big.

Chapter 8 - UNSHAKEABLE BEAUTY

Exercise #16 It starts with a decision

A beautiful thing is never perfect. - Egyptian Proverb

Let's review a couple of points from the book text:

- ◊ God sees us in the light of eternity – in the light of who He created us to be. He sees the promise and the potential that is inside of us. The beauty He sees in us lasts forever. He knows who we are at the core of our being – underneath all the layers and, He says that woman is good!
- ◊ Change and progress are messy. Moving into living an intentional life can be messy. It's ok – it's part of the journey.
- ◊ Excuses never won a race, a prize, or brought growth.
- ◊ The only way to begin to change is to begin. Just start. Identify one action you can take today, that is a step forward. There's a great quote by Arthur Ashe who puts it like this, "Start where you are, use what you have, do what you can".

My first action step that I will complete today is:

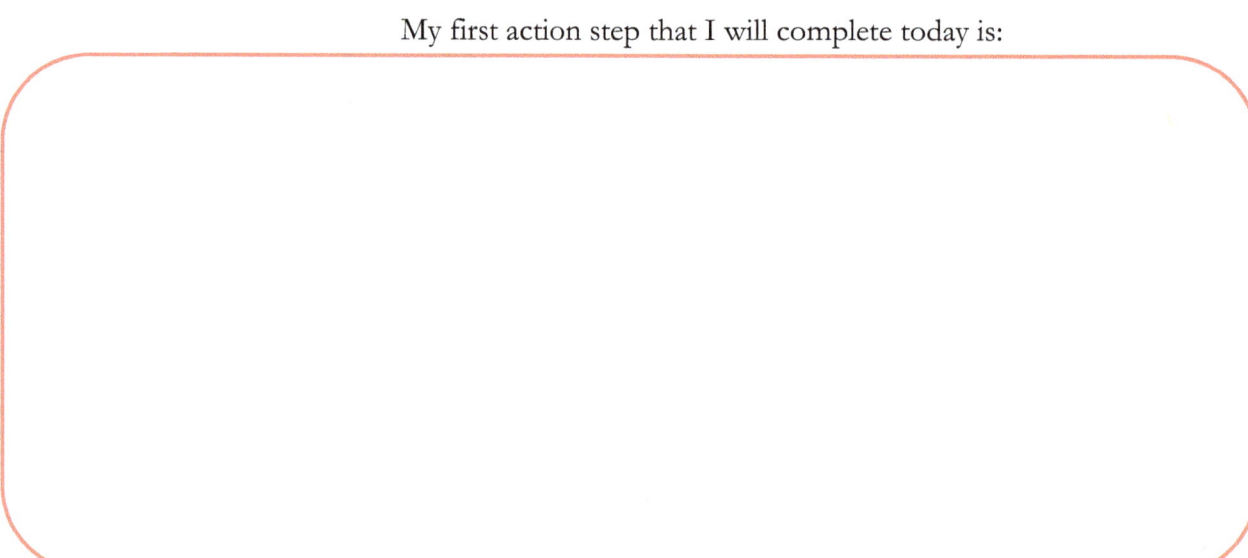

Set your mind – DECIDE that the shift starts now. You can have excuses, or you can get results. It really is that simple. Change isn't often easy, but it is simple. It's all in the power of the mind. Great athletes will tell you the difference between good and great is primarily mental. Two people of equal physical ability will not have the same results if one of them is mentally stronger. You can talk yourself into or out of succeeding. Our thought life plays a very significant part in making the commitment and keeping the commitment. They are two distinct efforts.

Making a commitment, even to yourself, can be tricky. You need a few guaranteed successes before you tackle a big change. Let's say your goal is to run a 5k race (3.2 miles) but you really haven't done much running since high school. You should not head out the door and expect to run 3 miles non-stop the first time out – that sets you up for failure and an entire carton of ice cream eaten in one sitting to console yourself. Just say NO!

Break it down into manageable steps so you get some momentum going. Here is an example of what I mean.

1. Your commitment to yourself is to run 3.2 miles. That is the end goal. To reach that goal, start slow and progressively run farther each week. (Look up couch-to-5K apps for your phone.)
    1. Your first incremental commitment is to plan and commit to walk-and-run at least 5 days a week.
        a. The smaller increment of commitment is to prepare your running gear ahead of time. Lay it out and have it handy so it is a no brainer and there is no time for excuses when it's time to hit the pavement.
        b. Already have water in a bottle that you can either sip on before you run or take with you.
    2. The second incremental commitment is to celebrate each accomplishment regardless of size. Just making it out the door and walking a couple of blocks is a win! Celebrating each achievement trains our brain to recognize the positive growth. Over time, you can celebrate bigger achievements with more gusto if you chose to. Just saying "Congratulations to me on my accomplishment!" out loud is a way of celebrating.
    3. The third incremental commitment is to report your progress to a friend. This is not just about accountability - - it is more about a shared experience being a validation that it happened and it's important enough to share with someone.

This is just an example of how you can set yourself up for a win. Use and re-use this approach each time you tackle something new. It does work!

Exercise #17 Kindness Matters

I have a vision of creating a worldwide kindness movement. It is the idea of a pebble dropping into a body of water and the ripples that act creates. If I am kind to you and you are kind to the next person you meet, and they continue the wave, we can create ripples across the entire country in a matter of weeks.

In the book, we defined kindness as:

Kindness is grace applied to someone or a situation where calling out a fault or flaw would be so easy to do.

The journal prompt in the book asked you to write down how you will create a kindness ripple. I want to take that farther if you are willing. <u>I challenge you to do 14 acts of intentional kindness over the next 7 days.</u> Here are just a few starter ideas – the possibilities are endless however!

1. Pay for the drink order behind you in line at the coffee shop
2. Over tip your waiter or server
3. Write an encouraging note to someone and send it in the mail. It will make someone's day to get an unexpected card that is not a bill!
4. Go out of your way to open the door for people and let them go before you.
5. Freely give compliments to total strangers.
6. Simply smile at people.
7. Genuinely ask the clerk waiting on you how their day has been – show interest in them as a person.
8. Send any amount of money to a friend or loved one just because they are wonderful. It's not about the $ amount – it's about the love in the note.
9. Bake your friend, spouse or children their favorite dessert just for fun.
10. This one requires more money so may not work for everyone but go to a thrift shop and look for a single parent buying clothes for their children and pay for their purchase. (We've done this anonymously and it is such a blessing not only for them but for you too.)
11. Call your local school and see if there are kids who can't afford lunches or have a bill owed for lunches and pay for it.
12. Offer to babysit for free for a parent who just needs a break.
13. Buy silk flowers at the dollar store along with a basket. Arrange the flowers and drop it off at a nursing home for a resident who doesn't get visitors or have family close by. You could include some candy or a puzzle book.
14. There have been many more people become homeless because of Covid. Buy socks, pillows and personal care items and donate to a local shelter. There is a huge need.

***It is awesome to enlist others to join this activity with you. Kindness can be caught – let's make it contagious!!

Final thoughts on kindness:
- ◊ Kindness shuts down judgment because judgment shuts down relationships. We are the human race, and we were designed and intended to be in fellowship with other people. When we judge others, we create the wrong kind of ripple.
- ◊ Be kind and teach others to do the same. If it is to be, it's up to me. Start a kindness ripple wherever you are. You will never regret being kind.

Chapter 9 - ABANDON THE UGLINESS

Exercise #18 Flying Blind

In the book, we looked at the Johari Window – here's a quick review.

We have 4 sides to our personality:
1. The part of me that I and everyone else sees – my public personality (Arena)
2. The part of me that everyone else sees but I don't (Blind Spot)
3. The part of me that only I see – the inner me (Facade)
4. The unconscious part of me (Unknown)

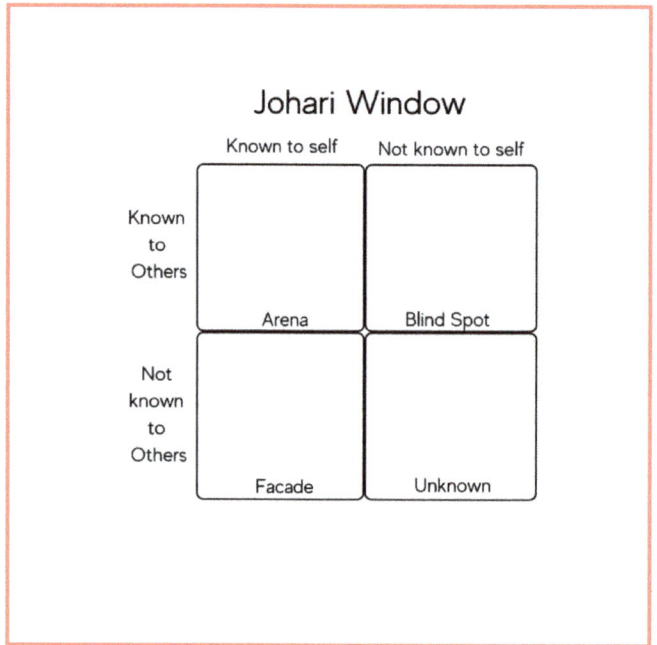

Our blind spots often trip us up and create conflict in our lives. However, we can also have positive aspects of ourselves that others see in us that we don't see in ourselves.

This assignment has 2 parts:
1. If you are on Social Media such as Facebook, Clubhouse, etc., make a post telling people you are doing research for an assignment and you need their help. Ask them for the top 2 things you are good at or that are your best qualities (see text below you can just copy). If not on social media, do the same thing with friends and family.
    o Suggested text: I am doing research for an assignment – can you help me out? What are 1 or 2 things I am good at or that are my best qualities that I may not realize about myself?

2. The flip side of that coin are the behaviors you have that create conflict with others, but you don't see – your blind side. I do not recommend posting this on social media. Instead ask people in your life who love you and genuinely want to see you grow – even if it's just one person. (see text below you can use for a script).
    - Suggested text: I am doing research for an assignment on my personal growth. Do you see behaviors or characteristics in me that you would call a blind spot? If there is more than one, what is the most frequent one you see?

The idea of both exercises is to begin getting insight into your blind spots. Here is a crucial point – <u>Do not overreact to any negative responses</u>! This is information to help you grow, not to berate yourself even more. Until you know there is a problem (if there is one), you cannot begin to change it. A simple example in my life was my gum chewing. I did not realize I had a habit of talking while I was chewing gum until I asked a question like this and someone was honest enough to give me the feedback.

Record your *positive* feedback here. What surprised you the most?

Record your *constructive* feedback here. What surprised you the most?

Chapter 10 - THE YOKE

Exercise #19 So many Rocks!

An exercise I do in one of my workshops is to use a black sharpie to write the burdens you are carrying on a literal rock and put it in a bag and feel the weight. We all have burdens, cares, regrets, emotions, memories, fear, and wrongs we've committed against others and they all create mental, emotional and spiritual weight. We carry the weight of other people's judgments, wrongs done to us, accidents, grief, disabilities and so much more.

Here is the image of a yoke from the book:

For this exercise, imagine that yoke across your shoulders and your buckets are filled with rocks imprinted with the words of all the weights you carry.

Here is a starter list to help you identify what your weights are:

BETRAYAL	HOPELESS	DREAMS DIED
DEATH	I KILLED SOMEONE	HELPLESS
SHAME	SINGLENESS	POVERTY
RAPE	LIED TO	ABANDONED
DIVORCE	INCEST	LONELY
CHRONIC ILLNESS	ADDICTION	BURDENED
INFERTILITY	PROCRASTINATION	PRIDE
LACK OF EDUCATION	FEEL INVISIBLE	ANGER
PHYSICAL ABUSE	OVERWEIGHT	UNFORGIVENESS
MENTAL ABUSE	FINANCES	REGRET
SEXUAL ABUSE	WAYWARD KID	DESPAIR
EMOTIONAL ABUSE	EATING DISORDER	VICTIM
HANDICAP	RESENTMENT	DISAPPOINTMENTS
"NO VALUE"	CANCER	DISILLUSIONED
"WORTHLESS"	DECEIVED	MENTAL ILLNESS

Take time to pray about your burdens and ask the Holy Spirit to help you identify them. Our subconscious likes to protect us and hide some of these so you may need to dig a little to find the heaviest ones. You do not have to identify all of them at once. For me, it took four or five times of doing this exercise to really uncover all of the big ones. I still find an occasional rock that I have to deal with.

My list of rocks in my buckets:

Once you have your list, even if it's one item or a dozen or more, take each word one at a time and pray the following prayer or something similar to release that burden.

> *Jesus, I bring you this burden that I am carrying named _____. I release to You all of the associated weight, negative emotions, negative memories, pain, hurt and damage it did to me and to my relationships. I ask that the blood that You shed on the cross would wash this away and separate it as far away from me as the East is from the West as Your word says (scripture). I release this to You and pray that it would no longer weigh me down or cause me any pain. Thank You for Your faithfulness to take this and carry it for me. In Jesus name, Amen.*

Once this is done for your list, again visualize your buckets being totally empty and the weight on the yoke being GONE! You have a new-found freedom. It may take a day or two to completely process the residue from the emotions, but they are gone for good.

Repeat this anytime you begin to feel overloaded and weighed down.

Chapter 11 - RESILIENCE

Exercise #20 Life is For Me

In the prior exercise, we just identified some of the rocks we carried in buckets across our shoulders. Many of those rocks were where life happened TO us instead of FOR us. We are resilient – we do and will bounce back. One way to do that is to reframe or redefine what happened to us into a gift that life gave us. (Yes, it can be a challenge at first to think this way.)

Pick 2 or 3 of the Rocks you released in Chapter 10. I would now like you to reframe the experience you had around that situation. What did you learn from that circumstance that you would not have otherwise learned? What strengths did you discover in yourself? What compassion do you have to give to others? Are there any ways you have benefited from your experiences? What lessons did you learn even though it was the hardest way to learn them? There are gifts in just about every situation that are the lessons we learn, the ability to help others in similar circumstances, and people that came into our lives in a good way because of the tough things we go through.

If a situation was very recent, it may be too soon to recognize the lesson or the gift that will come from it. Give yourself grace and time for those. It will come, it just may be in the future.

*Note: I certainly do recognize that not all situations can be directly of benefit and sometimes are really hard to deal with. It may be that simply surviving to live another day is the benefit you can identify right now.

For two or three of your rocks from Chapter 10, answer the following questions:
1. What benefit came to me or others?
2. What life lesson did this situation offer that I had not learned previously?
3. What strength(s) did I find in myself?

Rock #1: _____

Rock #2: _____

Rock #3: _____

Chapter 12 - PURITY OF HEART

Exercise #21 Motivated

I want to review some of the text from the book before we move to the exercise. Here are some key points:

- The Bible tells us that *"From the heart comes all of our words and motives"* (Matthew 12:34, Luke 6:45).
- When you're tired of being grumpy all the time and you don't like what the ugliness inside is doing to you, guess what?! You get to choose to change! This is where we have a heart-to-heart conversation with God and tell him we are wrong, ask for His help to change, and ask His forgiveness. In Psalms 51, King David put it this way, *"Create in me a clean heart, oh God, and renew a right spirit within me."*
- When we ask God for a new beginning and we mean it, God immediately starts things in motion to make changes for you – both inside and out. He will purify your heart, your motives, your attitude, and your outlook on life. Some of it will happen quite quickly, other parts over time.
- *"Blessed are the pure in heart for they shall **see** God."* (Matt 5:8) When you operate in that pure heart, you see God every day, everywhere, in everything. God's hand is on your life, guiding, providing, encouraging, and correcting. Beyond seeing God in everyday living, you will also hear His voice, feel the nudges of the Holy Spirit, and be blessed with His Presence always.
    - In this verse, the word "**see**" literally means 'to appear, to be seen, to behold'. It is possible to have an honest-to-goodness visitation from Jesus. Ask for it – seek it. He WANTS to have that level of relationship with you.

Our exercise is designed to promote your awareness of the motivations in your heart. Pure, selfless motivation is focused on doing good for all those around you – and that does include yourself. Self-focus motivation can be based on fear, scarcity, selfishness, immaturity and other lower vibrational emotions. Many of our motivations also have roots to them that stem from family cultures, church cultures, school lessons and also the school of hard-knocks.

Step 1. Ask the Holy Spirit to bring to your mind a time when you were purely motivated. It can be something very simple like giving someone a compliment about their outfit or buying someone an expected gift just because you love them. Feel how this affects you at all 3 levels – spirit, soul and body. Did you smile with the remembrance? Did your heart feel warm? Did you maybe chuckle a little bit even?

Record a few details about the situation and your reaction.

Step 2. Think about a time when your motives were not so clean and pure. You lied about something to protect yourself, you stole something, you gossiped about another person, you wrongly accused someone knowing it would get them in trouble. We can come up with these all day long. We all have bad motives sometimes. Again – note how this affected your body, soul and spirit. Do you see the contrast in the 2 situations?

Step 3. Ask God to help you develop a clean heart and pure motives. It will not occur overnight but is an 'over-time' evolution that will draw you closer to God and increase both your blessings in life and your ability to bless others.

Remember, you are not a tree – you can move if you don't like where you are today.

Part 3

BECOMING UNSHAKEABLE

Chapter 13 - IN STEP WITH THE HOLY SPIRIT

Part 3 of the book calls us into action. Let's Go!

Exercise #22 Why am I here?

If you grew up in church, it may have felt like it was so hard to "find God's will for your life". If you didn't grow up in church, you may have the same questions as to why you are here on earth, at this time in history. As an adult with a lot of years of walking with God, I have concluded we make it way too difficult and way too intellectual. When you are honest with yourself, deeply honest, you know what you are good at and what strikes passion in you. God made you exactly the way you are naturally with abilities, skills, and talents. He wants you to use those things to do good in the world, experience the joy of living and bring honor to Him.

List out at least 5 clues you have as to what your bigger purpose is in life. What makes you righteously angry? What fills your cup and brings true, deep satisfaction? What makes you excited to wake up tomorrow morning and do it again? What did you want to do/be as a child? This is often a clue for us. If you have a knowing or a nudge as to some part or all of your purpose, write that out as well.

Exercise #23 My Advocate

One of the Greek words for the Holy Spirit is 'Paraclete' which means counselor, advocate, comforter, or helper. It's important to know all the roles that Holy Spirit fills to empower us to understand how we can walk better with Him. The Holy Spirit reminds us that we are clean before God because of what Jesus did on the cross. The Holy Spirit will always remind us of what Jesus accomplished and that Jesus died for you. The Holy Spirit acts as our defense attorney with Satan in this sense. He advocates on our behalf and reminds Satan that we belong to God.

For this exercise, you need to research scriptures where God says you belong to Him. Ask the Holy Spirit to lead you to the right scriptures for you. There are different ways to find these scriptures.

Here are a few ideas.
1. Open your bible to wherever looks good and read both sides of the page. If you find a scripture that draws your attention, write it down here.
2. Go to your favorite web browser and search for "Scriptures of belonging to God" or something similar. Read 2 or 3 different lists and see which scriptures stand out to you and record them in this workbook.
3. Read Psalms 23, 24, 48, 73, 100, 119, or 139 and again look for verses that stand out or speak to you and record them here.

4. Use the verses you pick out as affirmations and commit them to memory. Speaking them out loud to yourself will help to settle them into your spirit.

Chapter 14 - SUBMIT AND SURRENDER

Exercise #24 What *do* I surrender?

I believe that if you are completing this workbook, you have a deep desire and hunger for more of God. What do you need to surrender to God in order to go all in? You know better than anyone else what is in-between you and Him. It can be attitudes, mindsets, addictions, idols, independence, fears, dreams, lusts and many, many more. My personal experience was God asking me to make a list of what I was willing to let go of and give over to Him. He told me it was all or nothing. He may ask the same of you or his request to you may be different. There are no right or wrong answers, just be truthful. I do have a caution - - be serious in this. If you are not ready to commit to something right now, don't put it down. You can always come back to this page later or make a commitment in your journal or just converse with Him.

Chapter 15 - WE ARE AN ENDANGERED SPECIES

Exercise #25 The Power of Agreement

… tremendous power is released through the passionate, heartfelt prayer of a godly believer! James 5:26 TPT

In our day and time, finding two people to agree on almost anything can be a challenge. We all have thoughts and opinions, and the trend of the day is to condemn anyone who thinks differently than we do. It creates discord and division, neither of which come from our Heavenly Father! What if we take a different, healthier, and more peaceful approach?

Prayer is a daily, ongoing conversation with the Father, Jesus, and the Holy Spirit. We are encouraged to "Pray always, without ceasing" (1 Thes 5:17). Talk to God when you're changing a diaper, changing your oil, washing dishes, running, running an errand, lifting at the gym, anytime and all the time. When you make every day an ongoing conversation with God, you grow close to Him. You learn to hear and recognize His voice. He talks to every one of us in a way that is significant to us. I often find that prayer is more listening than it is talking or asking. If I can be quiet and listen for the voice of the Holy Spirit – what some call The Still, Small Voice – I receive instruction, inspiration, answers, solutions, and questions to think about.

A powerful way to pray is to pray the bible over yourself, your family and friends, your finances, our nation and anything else that concerns you. Here is an example from Psalm 91;1-7. The title of this psalm is Safe and Secure.

Original Text	Personalized Text
When you abide under the shadow of Shaddai, you are hidden in the strength of God Most High.	When I abide under the shadow of Shaddai, I am hidden in the strength of God Most High.
He's the hope that holds me and the stronghold to shelter me, the only God for me, and my great confidence.	He's the hope that holds me and the stronghold to shelter me, the only God for me, and my great confidence.
He will rescue you from every hidden trap of the enemy, and he will protect you from false accusation and any deadly curse.	He will rescue me from every hidden trap of the enemy, and he will protect me from false accusation and any deadly curse.
His massive arms are wrapped around you, protecting you. You can run under his covering of majesty and hide. His arms of faithfulness are a shield keeping you from harm.	His massive arms are wrapped around me, protecting me. I can run under his covering of majesty and hide. His arms of faithfulness are a shield keeping me from harm.
You will never worry about an attack of	I will never worry about an attack of demonic

demonic forces at night nor have to fear a spirit of darkness coming against you.	forces at night nor have to fear a spirit of darkness coming against me.
Don't fear a thing! Whether by night or by day, demonic danger will not trouble you, nor will the powers of evil be launched against you.	Don't fear a thing! Whether by night or by day, demonic danger will not trouble me, nor will the powers of evil be launched against me.
Even in a time of disaster, with thousands and thousands being killed, you will remain unscathed and unharmed.	Even in a time of disaster, with thousands and thousands being killed, I will remain unscathed and unharmed.

When we pray this way, we are in alignment with God and in agreement with what He has already stated as truth. As we read and re-read these verses, it convinces our subconscious that we believe it and it becomes our truth as well. The psalms are always a good starting place to read and pray. In the New Testament, if you have a red-letter type of bible that shows the words that Jesus spoke, much of that text is also very powerful to pray over yourself.

The Bible also talks about the prayer of agreement between 2 or 3 people. In Matthew 18:20 it says, "For where two or three gather in my name, there am I with them.". There is extreme power in unity and agreement. If you and a couple of friends pray together in agreement with scripture, you will become Unshakeable! There is another scripture, Ecclesiastes 4:12, that says,

> *By yourself you're unprotected.*
> *With a friend you can face the worst.*
> *Can you round up a third?*
> ***A three-stranded rope isn't easily snapped.***

When you find like-hearted and like-minded friends and you agree in prayer, anything is possible!

Write out a favorite scripture or two by using personalization and then review these a few times a week.

Chapter 16 BECOMING

Exercise #26. God knows the how

"Every single second is an opportunity to change your life, because in any moment you can change the way you feel".
Rhonda Byrne

To change our world, we have to start with changing ourselves and those we have influence on.

I believe it is not possible to have a poverty or scarcity mindset AND accomplish all the things God has put me on earth to do. If I am going to impact my world for Christ and to spread the gospel, it takes finances, prosperity, and the right mindset and belief system. I held myself back for decades, waiting while I tried to figure it all out and determine the right "how". A friend used to have license plates that said, "Just Go". Once God has pointed you in a direction and you have a green light - - Just go! This is where Jesus told the disciples to GO into all the world and make more disciples. In this season, you get to partner with God and co-create with Him and fulfill the passion that He placed in you. This is where you find fulfillment, life satisfaction and you can say every day, "Life is beautiful".

We talked in Chapter Two of the book about being in the Flow of Heaven. When we are cooperating with God and in the place that He needs us to be, He already has provision figured out. However, in order to get us to the place we need to be with the right faith, mindset, and focus, He will use challenging circumstances to teach us reliance on Him. While God will never tempt us, He will try us to see if we're ready for the next bigger thing.

Take time, at least 20 minutes, to think back over the last several years at the challenges you've faced, the lessons that have come from them and then visualize how God is/could/may use those to help you become who you need to be for this next season of your life. There is space on this page and the next page.

Next, identify the places where you want to control the how of where you believe God wants to use you. The how can be things like finances, raw materials, networking with other people, an office, living in a different city, a skill set you feel you're missing, that you are not qualified, not smart enough, not *x* enough, too short, too tall, etc. These can look or feel like excuses, reasons and realistic shortcomings. However, we know, God doesn't call the qualified, He qualifies the called. In our weakness, He is strong and that is where we live in reliance on Him and His leading.

Finally, DREAM BIG! What immediately comes to your mind right now as you read this? Write it down without editing, leaving anything out or adjusting it. That flash you just saw in your mind is a clue if not more than that.

You are created exactly as God designed you, as He wanted and needed you to be in order to fill that piece of the puzzle that not one other person in all of time can do. You matter. Your life matters. Your contribution matters. Every single thing you need in the way of provision, wisdom, help, divine appointments, contacts, inventions, creativity – you name it – already exists. That inner nudge you're feeling right now is God as the Holy Spirit prompting you to move forward.

To live your life by design and not just by default, you have to be intentional. Your final assignment is to start TODAY, right now, living by intention and design. Write down a commitment to yourself and to God that starting today, you are moving forward into the purpose He called and created you for. Sign this, date it and I suggest posting it on your desk or somewhere visible as a reminder of your declaration.

Bibliography

1. Life Wheel, Adapted from Paul J. Meyer and Success Motivation Institute, 1960

2. Core Values Worksheet, created by Lysa Beltz, May 23, 2021

3. Luft, Joseph, and Ingham, Harrington. (1955). "The Johari window, a graphic model of interpersonal awareness". Proceedings of the Western Training Laboratory in Group Development. Los Angeles: University of California, Los Angeles.

4. Carroll, Lewis. Alice in Wonderland, first U.S. edition (the first printing of U.K. edition), 1865

5. Brewer, Troy, Numbers That Preach: Understanding God's Mathematical Lingo, Aventine Press (November 21, 2007)

Invitation to Connect

Congratulations! You completed the workbook and exercises, and you are well on your way to Becoming Unshakeable!

As the world continues to shake and be shaken, our light and our talents are needed more than ever before. We must step into our God-given dreams and callings and show the way to the hurting, lost and weary. The good is within us, especially with Jesus on board, and we GET to share that and influence all that we come in contact with. A simple smile to a stranger or a compliment to a cashier can shift their entire day and outlook. You are more powerful than you know and able to create ripple effects that you could never envision before. You are unshakeable!!

Since this is a .PDF, you can always print the exercises and do them again if one spoke to you now, and after you process for a while and grow, there is a new breakthrough you sense you need to find. These materials are available to you to use and re-use as long as you need to.

I would love to hear feedback on what you experienced, what worked and what didn't. You can post to me on Facebook, Instagram or email me at CoachLysa@LysaBeltz.com.

To keep up with all that is happening with *Becoming Unshakeable*, connect with me at:
Facebook: BecomingUnshakeable – community and group training
Website: http://www.lysabeltz.com/BecomingUnshakeable
Instagram: @CoachLysa

If you want to pursue your journey to Becoming Unshakeable *and* you need help, I am available for you. I offer personal prayer sessions and one-on-one life coaching on my website, http://www.lysabeltz.com/. I am also located on Facebook at Women Empowered 4 Life and Instagram at CoachLysa.

About the Author

Lysa, an Idaho native, has lived in Boise for most of her life. Lysa spent many years as a programmer/analyst and project manager in the corporate world. Her ability to build relationships with people and to help individuals and teams has served her exceptionally well. She brings that same approach to writing and building a relationship with her readers. Her goal is to help you realize your worth and live the life of peace and abundance you were created for.

Lysa has been married to her husband, Scott, for 33 years and has 3 daughters and sons-in-law, grandkids, grand-dogs, and 1 grand-cat. Scott and Lysa also have 3 dogs and a cat of their own, all of whom might be a little spoiled. Currently, all of the kids, pets, grandsons, and grand-animals live in the Boise valley.

Lysa met Jesus when she was 9 years old and has spent a lifetime getting to know Him and His heart for people. She has experienced marriage, divorce, re-marriage, a blended family, the ups and downs of relationships, scarcity, and also abundance. There have been very tough seasons and times of great blessing. Through it all, God has been her foundation and she has seen Him move in ways that can only be described as supernatural. In her books and her life, she uses what she has learned to help any and all that she touches with her faith.

Lysa is known for a warm, caring style and she has a passion to see each person succeed in being the person they were designed to be. Women Empowered 4 Life, the name of her personal empowerment company, perfectly describes Lysa's approach. It's that extra touch of empowerment, plus her ability to hold you accountable in achieving your goals, that makes the partnership so successful and the changes life-impacting.

Life is good when you are in the right place, at the right time, doing the right things!

Journaling Pages

"If we understood the power of our thoughts, we would guard them more closely. If we understood the awesome power of our words, we would prefer silence to almost anything negative. In our thoughts and words, we create our own weaknesses and our own strengths. Our limitations and joys begin in our hearts. We can always replace negative with positive." -Betty Eadie

Journaling Pages

" A journal is your completely unaltered voice."
Lucy Dacus

Journaling Pages

"Writing is medicine. It is an appropriate antidote to injury. It is an appropriate companion for any difficult change." – Julia Cameron

_____
_____
_____
_____
_____
_____
_____
_____
_____
_____
_____
_____
_____
_____
_____
_____
_____
_____
_____
_____
_____
_____
_____
_____
_____
_____
_____

Journaling Pages

"Your Journal is like your best friend, you don't have to pretend with it, you can be honest and write exactly how you feel"
— **Bukola Ogunwale**

Journaling Pages

"Your thoughts are the architect of your destiny." David O. McKay

www.ingramcontent.com/pod-product-compliance
Lightning Source LLC
Chambersburg PA
CBHW081842170426
43199CB00017B/2817